SUPER SKILLS

COOKING SKILLS

STEPHANIE TURNBULL

W
FRANKLIN WATTS
LONDON·SYDNEY

D0319234

An Appleseed Editions book

Paperback edition 2014

First published in 2012 by Franklin Watts
338 Euston Road, London NW1 3BH

Franklin Watts Australia
Hachette Children's Books
Level 17/207 Kent St, Sydney, NSW 2000

© 2012 Appleseed Editions

Created by Appleseed Editions Ltd,
Well House, Friars Hill, Guestling,
East Sussex TN35 4ET

Designed and illustrated by Guy Callaby
Edited by Mary-Jane Wilkins
Photo research by Su Alexander

ISBN 978 1 4451 3176 4

Dewey Classification: 641.5

All words in **bold** can be found in the Glossary on page 30.

Website information is correct at the time of going to press. However, the
publishers cannot accept liability for any information or links found on third-
party websites.

A CIP catalogue for this book is available from the British Library.

Picture credits
t = top, b = bottom, l = left, r = right, c = centre
Page 2l Argunova/Shutterstock, r Perutskyi Petro/Shutterstock; 3 Fotosutra.
com/Shutterstock; 4t Jupiterimages/Thinkstock, b Iwona Grodzka/
Shutterstock; 5bl Richard Peterson/Shutterstock, all other images Thinkstock;
6l Carlos Yudica/Shutterstock, r Alistair Cotton/Shutterstock; 8, 9, 10 & 11
Thinkstock; 12 Jupiterimages/Thinkstock; 14 Thinkstock; 15 Sevenke/
Shutterstock; 16 Thinkstock; 17l Monkey Business Images/Shutterstock,
r George Doyle/Thinkstock; 18 Eising/Thinkstock; 19 Thinkstock; 20 Dick Luria/
Thinkstock; 21 White78/Shutterstock; 22, 24 & 25 Thinkstock;
26 Jupiterimages/Thinkstock; 28t Nick White/Thinkstock, c & b Thinkstock;
29 & 30 Thinkstock; 31 Shutterstock

Front cover: Rido/Shutterstock

Printed in China

Franklin Watts is a division of Hachette Children's Books,
an Hachette UK company.
www.hachette.co.uk

CONTENTS

CLEVER COOKING

Do you want to cook fantastic food for yourself, your friends and your family? Many dishes look difficult, but are really quite simple if you have a few cooking skills. This book gives you the know-how to make all kinds of quick and easy snacks, meals and treats.

Getting started

Before you start cooking, gather all your ingredients and equipment. Items such as scales, measuring jugs and spoons, chopping boards, sharp knives, a colander, peeler and grater are essential. Some recipes also use a blender or hand-held liquidizer. Unless a recipe states otherwise, each one serves four people.

▲ Using the right utensils makes cooking much easier. Don't forget to wash up and put everything away afterwards.

HINTS AND WARNINGS

Boxes with a light bulb symbol contain handy hints for improving your skills.

Look out for exclamation marks, too – these boxes give safety warnings and other helpful advice.

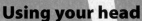

Using your head

Kitchens can be dangerous places. Here are some vital safety rules.

★ Be hygienic: tie back long hair, roll up sleeves, wear an apron and wash your hands before and after handling food. Work on a clean surface.

★ Use a separate knife and chopping board for raw meat. In the fridge, keep raw meat on a covered plate on the bottom shelf, where it can't touch other foods.

★ Watch your fingers when cutting and slicing with sharp knives. Concentrate!

★ Handle blenders and other equipment cautiously. Never touch them with wet hands.

★ Remember that ovens and stoves get very hot. Use oven gloves, beware of rising steam as you lift pan lids, and turn handles inwards so you don't knock them off the stove.

★ Don't keep leftover food for more than two days.

★ Always get help from an adult if you need it!

Likes and dislikes

When cooking for others, remember to check whether they are **vegetarian**, **vegan**, or have food **allergies**. Foods that can cause allergic reactions include milk, nuts, eggs, **soya**, wheat and shellfish. Other people have an intolerance to certain foods, which means that they feel ill after eating them. Read packet labels carefully to check what they contain.

ESSENTIAL SKILLS

Some basic cooking techniques come up again and again in recipes. Knowing them well saves you time, improves your cooking and gives you confidence to try more complicated recipes. Here are a few vital cooking skills.

Peeling

To peel foods such as carrots, first cut off the ends, then use a good, sharp peeler to slice off the peel in strips from top to bottom. Foods that don't need peeling must be washed well in a colander.

▲ *Peel away from your body so you don't risk injuring yourself with the peeler.*

Grating

Graters come in different shapes and sizes, but they all work the same way. Hold your grater firmly and slide the food up and down against the holes. It may help to rest the grater on a flat surface. Keep your fingers out of the way. If the food is too small to grate properly, chop it finely instead.

Chopping

When chopping a fruit or vegetable, cut it first so that it lies flat and doesn't slide around. Use a sharp knife, and don't try to chop too quickly. For foods with thick skins, such as tomatoes, peppers and aubergines, a **serrated** knife can grip the skin better. Chop into roughly bite-sized cubes, unless the recipe tells you differently. Bigger chunks may not cook through, and tiny pieces may turn to mush.

When grating lemon or orange zest (skin), stop when you reach the white layer, as it's very bitter.

Greasing

Baking sheets, tins and dishes need greasing to stop food sticking to them while cooking. Just smear some margarine or butter on a square of kitchen roll, then rub it all over the inside.

Kneading

Kneading is a way of mixing dough to make it rise when it cooks.

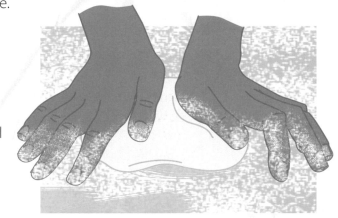

1. Place the dough on a floured surface. Put some flour on your hands, too.

2. Push a section of dough away from you with the heel of one or both hands.

3. Now pull it back with your fingers and fold it over itself. Turn the dough and repeat for about ten minutes, until it feels smooth and stretchy.

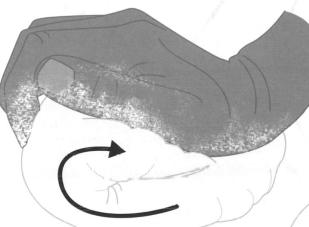

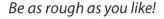

Be as rough as you like!

4. Test the dough by pressing your finger into it. It should slowly spring back.

Mixing

There are many different ways of mixing! Whisking means mixing very fast, usually with a hand whisk or fork, for example to make cream stiff. Creaming means blending sugar and butter until they are smooth and fluffy. Folding means combining ingredients very gently, usually so you don't beat all the air out of them.

hand whisk

Taste savoury dishes before you serve them to check the flavour. Adding a sprinkle of salt and pepper often improves the taste.

NO-COOK COOKERY

Quick and easy snacks, lunches and party food often don't involve cooking at all. Start with these simple recipes and test them out on your friends. As well as using fresh, healthy ingredients, you'll have plenty of chopping, grating and mixing practice!

▲ *Crunchy vegetables make a good alternative to crisps. Cut them into strips and serve with dips.*

Crunchy coleslaw

You can buy ready-made coleslaw, but your own will taste much better.

You will need:
- ★ *2 carrots*
- ★ *¼ white cabbage*
- ★ *¼ red cabbage*
- ★ *few sprigs parsley*
- ★ *6 tbsp natural yoghurt*
- ★ *2 tbsp mayonnaise*
- ★ *½ tsp mustard*
- ★ *1 lemon*

1. Peel the carrots and grate them into a large bowl. Carefully cut the white cabbage into thin slices. Do the same with the red cabbage. Chop the parsley sprigs and add everything to the bowl.

2. In a small bowl, mix the natural yoghurt, the mayonnaise, the mustard and a squeeze of fresh lemon juice. Add the mixture to the big bowl and stir to coat the vegetables.

3. If you want, add extra ingredients, such as apple slices, finely chopped red onion or spring onion, raisins, sliced radishes, pecans or walnut pieces. Pick and choose the things you like!

Don't make coleslaw more than a few hours ahead of time, otherwise the vegetables will lose their crunch.

You will need:

* ★ 200g smoked salmon
* ★ 1 small tub cream cheese
* ★ 1 lemon
* ★ chopped dill or parsley

Speedy salmon pâté

Make this quick smoked salmon **pâté** to serve alongside the coleslaw.

1. Chop the smoked salmon and put in a bowl. Add the cream cheese and squeeze over the juice of half a lemon.

2. Whizz everything together using a hand-held blender or food processor. Stop before the paste is completely smooth – leave some bits of salmon to add texture.

Hand-held blenders are great because you don't have to transfer food to a different container.

3. Add a few grinds of black pepper, then spread your pâté on toasted baguette slices or small crackers, or serve it as a dip. Sprinkle a little chopped dill or parsley on top.

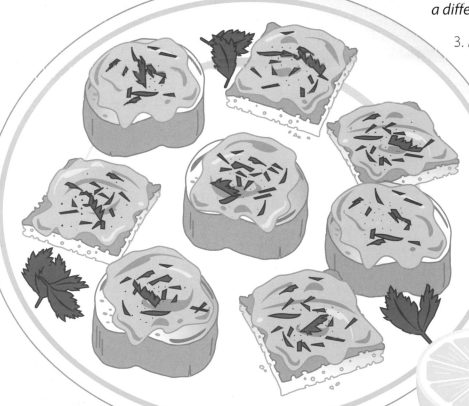

EASY MEALS

If you want to learn to cook, start with basic foods and everyday dishes. As you get more confident, add extra ingredients or try more complicated variations. Why not begin with baked potatoes or soup?

Super spuds

It's very easy to bake a potato. First, wash and scrub a large baking potato. Prick the skin with a fork then rub on a little sunflower oil – this will help the skin go crispy. Bake it at 200°C (180°C fan oven, 400°F, gas mark 6) for an hour. Push in a knife to check whether it's soft inside. If not, give it a bit longer.

Stuffed potatoes

Next, try stuffing a baked potato. Slice off the top, scoop out the pulp and mash it in a bowl with a blob of butter, a handful of grated cheese and a tablespoon of crème fraîche or sour cream. Spoon the mixture back into the skin, then put it back in the oven for a few minutes to heat through.

◀ *Create all kinds of delicious stuffed potatoes by adding different fillings, such as tuna, diced ham or chopped spring onions.*

Potatoes cook quickly in the microwave, but they won't have a crisp skin and don't taste so good. It's worth taking the time to bake them in the oven!

Soup ideas

Soups are fun as you can decide which ingredients to put into them. Create chunky soups by chopping vegetables, frying them gently in a large pan with a little oil, adding beef, chicken or vegetable **stock** and herbs and leaving them to **simmer** until the vegetables are soft.

▶ *Try including sweet potatoes and chick peas in a chunky soup.*

Easy peasy pea soup

If you want a smooth, puréed soup, try this simple recipe.

You will need:
- ★ 1 carrot
- ★ 1 stick celery
- ★ 1 onion
- ★ 1 tbsp olive oil
- ★ 1 stock cube
- ★ 400g frozen peas
- ★ small bunch of mint

1. Peel and slice the carrot, wash and slice the celery and peel and chop the onion.

2. Put a large pan on a medium heat and add the olive oil. Add the carrot, celery and onion and mix with a wooden spoon. Cook them for about five minutes.

3. Crumble a chicken or vegetable stock cube into a measuring jug and pour in a litre of boiling water from the kettle. Stir to dissolve the cube, then add the liquid to the pan.

4. Add the frozen peas, bring the soup to the boil and let it simmer for ten minutes. Take it off the heat.

5. Pick and wash the leaves from a small bunch of mint. Add them to the pan with a sprinkling of salt and pepper.

6. Purée the mixture with a hand-held liquidizer or blender until smooth. Heat it through, then serve. Try adding a handful of **croutons**, crumbled grilled bacon or a swirl of cream to each bowl.

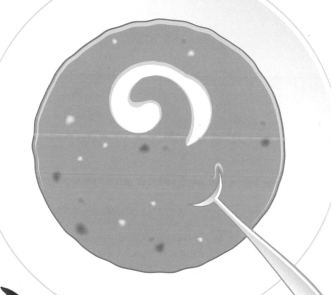

SUPER ★ FACTS

★ The Spanish soup gazpacho, which is served cold, contains raw vegetables and stale bread.

★ Chinese bird's nest soup really does contain a nest – but not twigs! Swifts make nests from saliva, which hardens as it dries. In soup, it dissolves into a gloopy liquid.

★ Soups can also be made with fruit and served as a dessert.

PERFECT PASTA

Some chefs spend hours mixing, rolling and cutting their own pasta, but don't worry – ready-made, dried pasta can taste just as good! It still takes practice to cook it just right. Follow these tips for perfect pasta dishes.

Cooking method

You need to cook dried pasta in a large pan of boiling, salty water. Allow 75g of pasta per person. Make sure the pasta is covered with water at all times, and stir it now and then to stop it sticking to the pan. Check the packet for how long to cook – usually 10-12 minutes. If you boil pasta for too long, it goes soggy.

You will need:

Meatballs
* ★ 6 cream crackers
* ★ 450g lean minced beef or pork
* ★ 1 tsp Dijon mustard
* ★ 1 tsp dried oregano
* ★ 1 egg

Sauce
* ★ 1 onion
* ★ 3 cloves garlic
* ★ 2 tbsp olive oil
* ★ 2 tins chopped tomatoes
* ★ 1 tbsp tomato purée
* ★ 1 tsp oregano
* ★ 5 basil leaves

Marinara meatball pasta

This fantastically filling meal has three parts: spaghetti, meatballs and a famous Italian tomato sauce called a marinara. Everything has to cook at once, so it will test your ability to multi-task – a skill all great chefs need!

1. Meatballs first: put the cream crackers in a clean plastic bag and crush them with a rolling pin. Tip the crumbs into a bowl and break up any last big pieces with your hands.

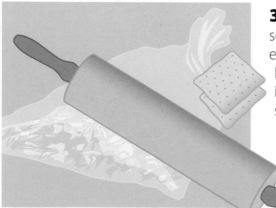

▲ *Pasta can be served hot with sauce, or cold in a salad.*

2. Add the minced beef or pork, the mustard, dried oregano, egg and a good sprinkling of salt and pepper.

3. With clean hands, scrunch and mix everything well. Divide the mixture into four equal-sized lumps.

4. Divide one lump in half, then split each half into three. Shape each small piece into a meatball. Do the same with the other big lumps, so you end up with 24 meatballs. Cover the bowl with cling film and put it in the fridge.

6. Add the chopped tomatoes, tomato purée and a sprinkle of salt and pepper. Wash and finely chop the basil leaves and add them with the dried oregano.

Mind your fingers when chopping the basil.

5. For the sauce, chop the onion and finely slice the garlic. Add extra cloves if you really like garlic! Put everything in a large pan with the olive oil, and fry on a medium heat for about five minutes.

Stir with a wooden spoon so they don't burn.

7. Mix everything well and simmer gently, with the lid on, for about 25 minutes.

8. Heat a large pan of water to boiling point, then add 75g spaghetti per person.

9. At the same time, cook the meatballs in olive oil in a frying pan. Turn them with a spatula every few minutes. They will take around ten minutes to cook through. Check they're done by cutting one open – if it's still pink, it's not ready.

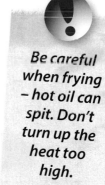

Be careful when frying – hot oil can spit. Don't turn up the heat too high.

10. When everything is cooked, drain the spaghetti in a colander and serve in bowls or on plates. Put the meatballs in the sauce, mix and spoon on top of the spaghetti.

SPEEDY STIR FRIES

Stir fries are the ultimate fast food – bite-sized pieces of meat and vegetables cooked at top speed over a high heat in a big pan called a wok. If you don't have a wok, you can use a large pan.

▲ *A wok has a rounded shape that makes it easier to mix and toss the stir fry as it cooks.*

You will need:

* ★ 75g dried egg noodles per person
* ★ 2 skinless chicken breasts
* ★ 1 onion
* ★ 2 cloves garlic
* ★ thumb-sized piece root ginger
* ★ handful mangetout
* ★ small tin water chestnuts
* ★ 1 tbsp sunflower oil
* ★ 2 handfuls beansprouts
* ★ 3 tbsp soy sauce
* ★ 2 tbsp sweet chilli sauce

Timing tips

The key to stir frying is good timing. Prepare the ingredients beforehand, as they cook quickly in a wok, and you need to keep stirring. Add the ingredients that take longer to cook first – for example, don't throw in bean sprouts before chicken, or they'll be soggy by the time the meat is ready!

Chicken chow mein

Adding noodles to a stir fry creates a dish called chow mein. This recipe uses chicken, but you could try prawns or **tofu** instead.

1. Boil a large pan of water. Add about 75g of dried egg noodles per person and cook them according to the packet instructions – about four minutes. Drain in a colander and set aside.

2. On a chopping board, cut the chicken breasts into thin, finger-length strips with a sharp knife.

3. Using a clean knife and chopping board, thinly slice the onion and garlic cloves, and peel and finely chop the root ginger. Wash the mangetout and halve them lengthways. Drain and halve the water chestnuts too.

4. Now you're ready to start stir frying. Heat a wok over a medium heat, then add a swirl of oil and the chicken strips. Cook for about five minutes.

Stir with a spatula so the meat doesn't stick.

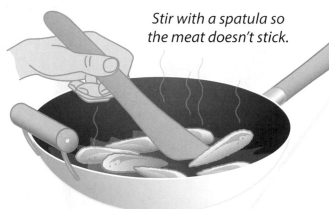

5. Add the onion, garlic and ginger and stir fry for another two minutes.

6. Now add the water chestnuts, bean sprouts and noodles. Mix in the soy sauce and the sweet chilli sauce.

Many supermarkets sell sweet chilli sauce – or try oyster sauce instead.

Stir fries look best when they are colourful. Try mixing baby sweetcorn with broccoli florets, carrot sticks and red pepper strips.

7. When everything is piping hot, serve in bowls and eat straight away.

 SUPER ★ FACTS

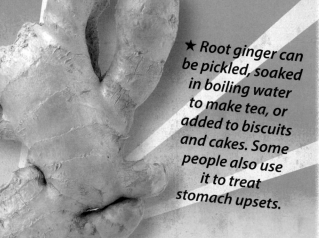

★ Soy sauce is made from soya beans and salt, and has been used for more than 2,000 years in east and south-east Asian cooking.

★ Some enormous woks are designed for cooking on outdoor stoves. Chefs use giant paddles to mix stir fries for hundreds of people at once!

★ Root ginger can be pickled, soaked in boiling water to make tea, or added to biscuits and cakes. Some people also use it to treat stomach upsets.

BRILLIANT BURGERS

Burgers in bread rolls are great for parties, barbecues, and any time you don't want to bother with knives and forks! Shop-bought burgers can be full of fat and not very satisfying, so it's much better to make your own.

Beefburgers

For beefburgers, use the meatball recipe on page 12 and mould the mixture into six round, flat shapes, about 2 cm thick. Cook them in a frying pan for about four minutes each side. Serve them in bread rolls with lettuce, sliced tomato or grated cheese.

You will need:
* ★ 2 tins chickpeas
* ★ 1 red onion
* ★ 2 cloves garlic
* ★ handful flat leaf parsley
* ★ 1 tsp ground coriander
* ★ 1 tsp ground cumin
* ★ ½ tsp chilli powder
* ★ l tsp lemon juice
* ★ 2 tbsp plain flour
* ★ 1 tbsp sunflower oil
* ★ rocket, cucumber, roasted red pepper strips
* ★ 4 burger buns

Falafel burgers

Falafel is a Middle Eastern food made from chickpeas. It's a great alternative to meat and is high in **protein** and low in fat.

1. Drain the chickpeas and pat dry with kitchen roll.

2. Roughly chop the red onion, garlic cloves and parsley.

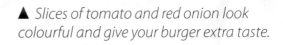

▲ *Slices of tomato and red onion look colourful and give your burger extra taste.*

3. Put the chickpeas and chopped ingredients in a blender. Add the ground coriander, ground cumin, chilli powder, lemon juice and plain flour. Don't forget a sprinkle of salt and pepper.

6. While this is cooking, rinse the basmati rice in a sieve under cold water. Bring 600 ml water to the boil in a pan and add the rice. Stir and simmer with a lid on for 15 minutes.

7. Serve the curry with desiccated coconut sprinkled over the top.

Not all curry powders contain the same ingredients, and some are hotter than others. Always check what it says on the jar!

Spiced up rice

Try turning rice a fantastic yellow colour by adding a teaspoon of **turmeric** as it simmers. You could also heat a blob of butter in a frying pan and add a handful of flaked almonds and a handful of sultanas. Fry them gently for a minute until the sultanas swell up, then mix them into the cooked rice with a fork.

▲ You can also flavour rice by adding a few cloves or spicy seed pods called cardamoms.

BAKING BASICS

Baking means making bread, cakes and other oven-cooked foods. It's a tricky skill to perfect, as you need to weigh and measure ingredients precisely, and get the cooking time just right. The key is to stick to simple recipes at first, and follow them carefully.

You will need:

* ★ *450 kg bread flour*
* ★ *300 ml warm water*
* ★ *1 sachet dried yeast*
* ★ *1 tbsp olive oil*
* ★ *1 tsp salt*

Don't use hot water, or the yeast won't work.

Bread for pizza

A fun way to start baking is to make bread dough for pizza bases.

1. Sieve the flour into a large mixing bowl. Add the salt and dried yeast. Make a hollow in the middle and pour in the warm water and olive oil.

2. Mix into a smooth dough with a wooden spoon. Add a few drops of water if it's dry, or a sprinkling of bread flour if it's sticky.

3. Now put the dough on a floured board and knead for about ten minutes (see page 7), until it feels smooth and stretchy.

4. Put the dough back in the bowl and cover with a tea towel. Stand it in a warm place for about an hour and a half. The yeast will make the dough double in size during this time.

5. While the dough rises, make the marinara sauce from page 13 – but just use one tin of tomatoes. Simmer for about half an hour, so it's nice and thick, then leave it to cool.

6. Divide the dough into four pieces and roll out each one on a floured surface. Make them circular and about 1 cm thick. Lay them on greased baking trays. Heat the oven to 220°C (200°C fan oven, 425°F, gas mark 7).

7. Smooth a large tablespoon of the sauce over each base, then cover with thin slices of mozzarella cheese. Add a mixture of toppings (be creative!) and finish with grated cheddar cheese.

You could try:

A pepperoni, onions and green pepper

B smoked ham and pineapple

C mushrooms, olives and tomato

8. Cook the pizzas for about 12 minutes, until the edges are golden and the cheese is melting. Be careful not to overcook and burn them.

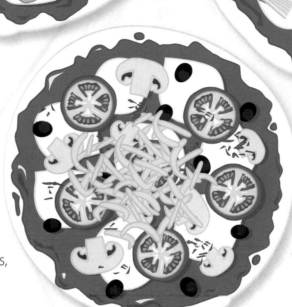

A

B

C

▲ *Italian mozzarella cheese is ideal for pizzas as it goes gooey and stretchy when cooked.*

For a party, make the bases and sauce beforehand and store in the fridge. When friends arrive, spread the sauce and put out bowls of different toppings, so everyone can create their own pizza.

Bread rolls

To make bread rolls, follow steps 1 to 4, then knead the dough for a few minutes and divide it into eight balls. Put the rolls on a greased baking tray and leave to rise again for 20 minutes. Brush with milk and sprinkle with plain flour, then bake in a preheated oven at 200°C (180°C fan oven, 400°F, gas mark 6) for 10-15 minutes, until the rolls are golden brown on top.

DELICIOUS DESSERTS

Every good cook needs a few really great dessert recipes up their sleeve, so here are two classic dishes to try. Remember that they're very sweet and filling, so they're best saved for special occasions when you really want to wow your friends and family.

You will need:

* ★ 1 packet digestive biscuits
* ★ 75g butter
* ★ 475g cream cheese
* ★ 100g icing sugar
* ★ 1 lime
* ★ 1 tsp vanilla essence
* ★ 200 ml double cream
* ★ 3 tbsp water

Lime cheesecake

This cheesecake tastes great – and, best of all, it doesn't involve any cooking. It's worth buying a springform cake tin with a separate base, otherwise you'll have trouble removing your finished cheesecake.

1. Crush 13 biscuits into fine crumbs with the end of a rolling pin or your fingers.

separate base

5. Ease the cheesecake out of the tin and top with sliced fruit or a fruit compote (see page 24). It will serve about eight people.

2. Melt the butter in a pan, add the crumbs and stir. Grease the tin, spoon in the biscuit base and press flat. Put in the fridge for an hour.

3. Put the cream cheese in a large bowl. Add the icing sugar and cream it with a wooden spoon. Grate in the zest of a lime, then squeeze in the juice. Stir in the vanilla essence.

4. In another bowl, whisk the double cream until it starts to thicken. Gently stir it into the mixture, a few spoons at a time. Empty the mixture into the cake tin, spread it evenly, and refrigerate for at least an hour.

Speedy treacle pud

No one will believe that this pudding takes seven minutes to cook! The secret is using a microwave.

You will need:
★ 100g butter
★ 100g caster sugar
★ 2 eggs
★ 2 tbsp milk
★ 100g self-raising flour
★ 1 orange
★ 8 tbsp golden syrup

1. Cream the butter and sugar in a mixing bowl.

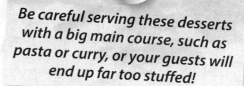

Be careful serving these desserts with a big main course, such as pasta or curry, or your guests will end up far too stuffed!

2. In a separate bowl, whisk the eggs and milk, then stir into the butter and sugar mixture.

3. Sieve in the flour and mix. Add the grated zest of an orange, then squeeze in the juice of half the orange.

4. Draw around the top of a large microwave dish on greaseproof paper. Cut out the circle.

5. Grease the dish, and spoon in the golden syrup. Pour the pudding mixture on top. Grease the circle of paper and put it, butter side down, on top.

6. Bake in a microwave for seven minutes on medium power, then leave to stand for a few minutes. Remove the greaseproof paper, put a plate on top of the dish and turn everything upside down so the pudding falls on to the plate. Serve with custard.

FRUIT FEASTS

Fruit is perfect if you want to finish your meal with a lighter dessert. Try making a fruit salad with your favourite fruits – and experiment with a few you've never tried before. How about lychees, mangoes, dragon fruit or ugli fruit? See what you can find in the shops!

You will need:

* 450g mixed berries
* 2 tbsp caster sugar
* 3 tbsp water
* granola
* ice cream

Berry compotes

A compote is a sweet fruit purée. Compotes are often made with berries such as raspberries, blackberries, strawberries and blueberries.

Create smoothies by mixing chopped fruit in a blender. Add milk or plain yoghurt for a creamier drink, or a tablespoon of honey as a sweetener.

1. Rinse the berries in a colander and heat them gently in a large pan with the caster sugar and water.

2. Once the mixture is simmering, remove from the heat and strain through a sieve to remove seeds and other bits.

3. In a tall glass, create layers of compote, ice cream and crunchy granola. This kind of dessert is called a sundae.

Use Greek yoghurt instead of ice cream for a breakfast dish.

Baked spiced apples

One of the tastiest hot fruit desserts is a baked apple.
Use cooking apples, or any large, slightly tart eating apples.

You will need:

* ★ 4 large apples
* ★ 4 tbsp dark brown sugar
* ★ 1 tsp mixed spice
* ★ handful sultanas
* ★ handful chopped pecans or walnuts
* ★ 4 tsp butter or margarine

1. Preheat the oven to 200°C (180°C fan oven, 400°F, gas mark 6). Wash four large apples and remove the cores. Stand them in a shallow baking dish.

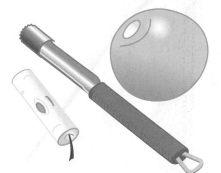

Use an apple corer.

2. In a small bowl, mix the dark brown sugar, mixed spice, sultanas and chopped pecans or walnuts.

3. Fill the apples with the mixture and sprinkle any extra around the dish. Put a teaspoon of butter or margarine on top of each apple and pour a little water into the dish – make it about 5 mm deep.

4. Put on a low shelf in the oven and bake for 15 minutes, then remove and spoon some of the syrupy liquid on top of the apples to keep them moist. Put back in the oven for another 10-15 minutes. Serve with the juice poured on top.

★ There are more than 7,500 types of apple worldwide.

★ Pineapples are a type of berry. They got their name because they look like pine cones.

SUPER ★ FACTS

★ Some wild bananas are pink, red, or have green and white stripes. Some are very fat and others are shorter than your little finger!

SWEET SNACKS

Treats such as buns and biscuits are fun to make and ideal for parties and picnics – or even to wrap in a gift box and give as a present. Here are a couple of useful recipes to start you off.

You will need:
- ★ *125g butter*
- ★ *55g sugar*
- ★ *180g plain flour*
- ★ *55g choc chips*

Choc chip shortbread

Shortbread is a very simple, buttery biscuit. Here's an easy shortbread recipe, which you can make without the chocolate chips if you prefer.

1. Heat the oven to 170°C (150°C fan oven, 325°F, gas mark 3). In a bowl, cream the butter and sugar.

2. Stir in the plain flour and mix to a smooth dough, then stir in the chocolate chips.

3. Shape the dough into a fat sausage, wrap it in cling film and chill in the fridge for 20 minutes.

4. Cut the dough into thick rounds and arrange on a greased baking tray. Cook for 10-15 minutes until they're a pale golden colour. Carefully move them on to a wire rack to cool.

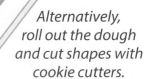

Alternatively, roll out the dough and cut shapes with cookie cutters.

Fruity bran muffins

These fantastic muffins are low in fat, full of fruit and use bananas instead of lots of sugar. Just remember to make the muffin mixture well in advance, so that the bran and fruit have plenty of time to soften and swell up.

1. Put the bran cereal, dried apricots and cranberries into a large bowl.

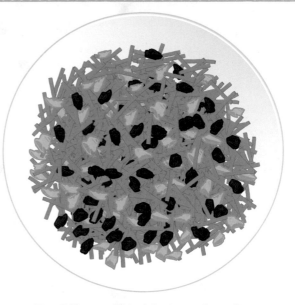

Try different dried fruit, such as figs or dates, and add chopped nuts, too.

2. Add the sugar and golden syrup. Pour over the skimmed milk and mix well. Cover the bowl and refrigerate for a few hours or overnight.

3. Heat the oven to 170°C (150°C fan oven, 325°F, gas mark 3). Mash the bananas and stir them into the mixture, along with the flour.

4. Spoon into a greased muffin tin and bake for about 15 minutes, until the muffins have risen and are golden brown. Remove them carefully and leave to cool on a wire rack.

The mixture makes about 24 muffins, so you may need to cook them in several batches. Save some by freezing a batch once they've cooled.

Temperatures and times for baking vary hugely with different ovens. Experiment to find out how long biscuits and buns take to brown in your oven.

WHAT NEXT?

The key to improving and expanding your cooking skills is to keep cooking! Search for recipes online and in the library, or ask relatives for their tried and tested favourites. Don't be afraid to experiment with ingredients or make up your own variations on recipes – after all, that's how celebrity chefs got started!

World food

Be open-minded when it comes to trying recipes. Look at dishes from other countries – how about Caribbean **jerk chicken**, Thai curry, Japanese **sushi** (below), Spanish **paella** or Moroccan **tagine**? If you go abroad, make a note of tasty ingredients and look for them at home.

Home growing

Herbs such as basil, thyme and mint are easy to grow in pots on your windowsill or outside. If you have space, try making a small vegetable garden. Cooking with ingredients you've grown yourself is very satisfying – and saves money, too.

▲ *Restaurant chefs plan dishes carefully, using a wide range of ingredients.*

For a professional touch, make sure your food is attractively presented. Use small *garnishes*, such as a sprig of coriander on a curry, or a sprinkling of icing sugar or chopped nuts on a cake.

▼ *Cake decorators use special icing to cover cakes and create delicate, complicated features such as flowers.*

Taking it further

It helps to learn from an expert, so find out whether there are any cookery classes or holiday workshops in your area. If you're serious about cooking as a career, look up college and university courses. Cook for friends and ask for their honest opinion – but be prepared to take criticism!

▲ *These clever rose sculptures are carved out of a melon and carrot pieces.*

Careers in food

If you have the skills and stamina to work in a hot, busy kitchen, you could become a chef, and even end up running your own restaurant. Or how about training as a butcher, baker or cake decorator? Perhaps you could be a nutritionist, advising people on healthy foods, or even an artist who makes food sculptures!

GLOSSARY

allergy
An extreme sensitivity to something, which usually leads to reactions such as sneezing and skin rashes, or sometimes even dizziness and difficulty breathing.

crouton
A small crunchy cube of baked or fried bread. You can try making your own croutons, or buy them in packets.

garnish
A small piece of food used to decorate and add extra flavour to a dish.

jerk chicken
A dish of chicken coated in hot spices and grilled or barbecued to give it a strong smoky flavour.

naan
A flat bread from south and central Asia. Some types of naan have fillings such as raisins, nuts, onions or minced meat.

paella
A dish made by simmering rice, stock, herbs and vegetables, plus seafood or meat.

pâté
A paste of finely minced meat.

protein
A substance found in animals and plants that is vital for building cells in your body and keeping bones, muscles, skin and other body parts strong and healthy.

serrated
A blade with notches, or teeth, like a saw.

simmer
To keep a liquid cooking gently at just under boiling point. First heat the liquid until it boils, then turn down the heat until there are hardly any bubbles.

soya
An east Asian plant that produces edible beans, used to make foods such as soya milk, tofu and soy sauce.

stock
Water flavoured with meat, vegetables, herbs or spices. Some cooks simmer their own stock, but the easiest method is to dissolve dried stock cubes in hot water.

sushi
Cooked rice combined with ingredients such as seafood, vegetables and seaweed.

tagine
A slow-cooked stew made in a big clay pot with a lid.

tofu
A food made from soya beans and water, pressed into blocks that look like white cheese. Tofu can be used in savoury and sweet dishes.

turmeric
A south Asian plant that is dried and ground into a peppery, orange powder.

vegan
Someone who doesn't eat any food that comes from animals, including meat, eggs and dairy products.

vegetarian
Someone who doesn't eat meat. Some vegetarians avoid other animal products, too.

USEFUL WEBSITES

www.activitytv.com/cooking-with-kids
Browse through lots of fun and easy recipes and watch
helpful videos showing you how to make each one.

www.vegetarian.about.com
Find all kinds of delicious vegetarian recipes and learn
more about vegetarian diets.

www.recipes.howstuffworks.com/tools-and-techniques/how-to-garnish-cooking.htm
Try fun and fancy ways of peeling, cutting and sculpting food to create amazing
edible decorations.

www.careerplanning.about.com/library/quiz/career_quizzes/blchef_quiz.htm
Answer a quiz to discover whether you have the right skills to become a chef,
then find out more about career options in cookery.

www.beyondbakedbeans.com
Learn useful basic cooking skills and try some straightforward
recipes. This site is aimed at students, so it also has helpful hints
for saving money on ingredients.

www.bbc.co.uk/food/techniques
Watch pretty much every food preparation technique you
can think of, from chopping an onion to filleting a fish!

INDEX